Critical Thinking

Liz Brown

WEIGL PUBLISHERS INC.

Published by Weigl Publishers Inc.
350 5th Avenue, Suite 3304, PMB 6G
New York, NY 10118-0069

Website: www.weigl.com

Library of Congress Cataloging-in-Publication Data

Brown, Liz (Elizabeth A.)
  Critical thinking / Liz Brown.
      p. cm. -- (Social studies essential skills)
  Includes index.
  ISBN 978-1-59036-755-1 (library binding : alk. paper) -- ISBN 978-1-59036-756-8 (soft cover : alk. paper)
  1. Critical thinking--Study and teaching. 2. Reasoning--Study and teaching. I. Title.
  LB2395.35.B76 2007
  370.15'2--dc22

                              2007024267

Printed in the United States of America
1 2 3 4 5 6 7 8 9 0 11 10 09 08 07

Editor: Heather C. Hudak
Design: Terry Paulhus

Table of Contents

What is Critical Thinking?

Critical thinking is the process of improving the way a person thinks about a subject, statement, or idea. When people use critical thinking skills, they are thinking about the way they think. To do this, they must identify, **evaluate**, compare, and **summarize** information.

Using critical thinking, people can make better decisions and find solutions to difficult problems. Critical thinkers can also tell if the information they have is truthful and accurate. This helps them form solid opinions and beliefs.

People who think well understand the outcome of their decisions and how their choices will affect their lives.

Using Open-ended Questions

Critical thinking skills are useful when you need to find answers to open-ended questions. Open-ended questions are questions that have more than one right answer. They often require further research and thought. Read the following passage and the questions that follow. Identify if any of the questions are open-ended. Then, answer the questions.

Abraham Lincoln was born on February 12, 1809, on a farm in Kentucky. His family lived in a one-room log cabin on the frontier. When Lincoln was two years of age, the family moved to a larger farm. When he was nine years old, his mother died from drinking poisoned milk. A year later, Lincoln's father remarried a widow with three children. Lincoln and his  *older sister attended school off and on. Lincoln later figured that he probably only attended one full year of school. His parents could not read or write.*

1. When was Lincoln born?
2. Did Lincoln live in a cabin as a child?
3. Lincoln only attended one year of school. How do you think this affected his work as president of the United States?
4. How did Lincoln's mother die?

Identifying Important Information

When looking for solutions to a problem, critical thinkers must recognize or identify what information is important and will help them reach a **conclusion**.

While reading and listening, there are signs that tell the reader or listener what to look for. Important points are often repeated. They are usually summarized at the end of a reading or presentation. In a textbook, the title of a chapter or section can give hints about the main ideas of the text. An author often presents important information in the first few sentences.

Read the passage below, and look for clues to help you identify the most important pieces of information.

In 1776, members of the Second Continental Congress decided to write an official statement of independence from Great Britain. This came to be known as the Declaration of Independence. Thomas Jefferson did the actual writing of the Declaration. The Declaration of Independence is an important document in the history of the United States. It declared the 13 colonies separate from Great Britain. Congress approved the Declaration on July 4, 1776. Today, Americans celebrate Independence Day on July 4.

Identifying the Point of a Passage

Identifying the point or message of a passage will help you decide what pieces of information are important. To do this, make a list of the most important points of information. Be alert for signs, such as repetition, that show a piece of information is important.

George Washington—First President of the United States
George Washington was the first president of the United States. His family was very wealthy and owned much land in Virginia. Before Washington became president, he was commander in chief of the Continental Army. This army fought against the British during the **American Revolution**.
In 1781, Washington met with other politicians at the Constitutional Convention in Philadelphia. This convention led to the creation of the United States and the **Constitution**. *When the convention was over, Washington's colleagues elected him as the first president of the United States. Washington took his* **oath** *of office on April 30, 1789.*

Evaluating Information

Once critical thinkers have identified the most important information in a passage, they must ensure that the information is true and without **bias**.

When reading and listening, a critical thinker must be able to tell if the information presented is a fact or an opinion. A fact is something that is true for everyone. It does not change, and it can be proven. An opinion is a view that a person has about a topic. Opinions change from person to person, and they are not always true. Statements that are opinions often contain descriptive words. The example below will help you tell the difference between a fact and an opinion.

Fact: Thomas Jefferson was elected as the third president of the United States.

Opinion: Thomas Jefferson was the greatest president in the history of the United States.

Fact: Thomas Jefferson was born on April 13, 1743.

Opinion: Thomas Jefferson was a handsome man.

Fact Versus Opinion

Look at the list of statements below. Determine which ones are fact and which ones are opinions. In your notebook, explain why you made the choices you did.

Thomas Jefferson wrote the Declaration of Independence in 1776.

The Declaration of Independence is difficult to read.

Fifty-six men signed the Declaration of Independence.

The men who signed the Declaration of Independence were the most important people in the United States.

The neatest signature on the Declaration of Independence is John Hancock's.

The first signature on the Declaration of Independence is John Hancock's.

Categorizing Information

Categorizing is the act of organizing information into groups according to similarities. Doing this helps critical thinkers better understand the information that is being presented.

Information can be grouped using paragraphs, charts, and graphs. Items of information can be placed in more than one category. For example, George Washington could be grouped into a category about presidents and also a category about the American Revolution.

The White House

The Capitol

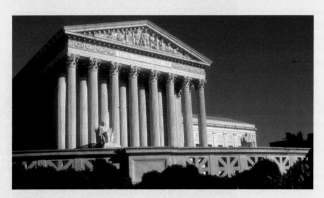

The Supreme Court

Categorizing helps critical thinkers understand how information is related. Can you think of one or more categories all of these buildings could fit into? One category might be government. Can you think of another one? Think about where all of these buildings are located.

Organizing Information

Look at the two text boxes. The top box contains a list of words about the creation of the United States. The bottom box has a list of categories that these words can fall into. You may have to look up some of the people, places, and events to know which category they belong to.

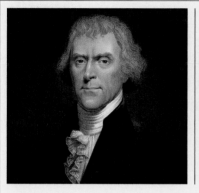

The Pennsylvania Packet, and Daily Ad

[Price Four-Pence.] WEDNESDAY, September 19, 1787.

WE, the People of the United States, in order to form
a more perfect Union, establish Justice, insure
Tranquility, provide for the common Defence, promote the General Welfare, and secure the Blessings of
Liberty to Ourselves and our Posterity, do ordain and establish this
Constitution for the United States of America.

List of Words

George Washington	American Revolution	documents
Thomas Jefferson	England	Benjamin Franklin
Boston Tea Party	Independence Hall	Constitution
Bill of Rights	King George III	U.S. flag

Categories

People	Places	Events	Things

Do any words fit into more than one category? Can you think of any other categories that some of these words can fit into?

Comparing and Contrasting Information

A critical thinker must compare and contrast many different pieces of information. Comparing and contrasting is thinking about how two or more things are alike and how they are different.

One reason that critical thinkers compare and contrast is to evaluate different facts or opinions. For example, by comparing and contrasting, a critical thinker can form his or her own opinions about a subject. In the box below is an example of how someone might compare and contrast two important figures in U.S. history using a **graphic organizer**.

Person	Similarities	Differences
George Washington	• worked as a politician • signed the Declaration of Independence • did not want Great Britain to rule America	• born in Virginia • was an army leader • served as president of the United States
Benjamin Franklin	• worked as a politician • signed the Declaration of Independence • did not want Great Britain to rule America	• born in Massachusetts • was a scientist, inventor, and writer • was president of the executive council of Pennsylvania

Making a Comparison Chart

Make a comparison chart like the one on the previous page. Compare two subjects you study at school or two television shows that you like to watch. What is similar about the two subjects or shows? What is different? Has comparing and contrasting changed your opinions in any way?

Summarizing Information

Critical thinkers must be able to summarize information. Summarizing is the ability to condense a large amount of information into a few main points. It helps critical thinkers develop a clear understanding of what they are learning and forming opinions about.

Summaries can be oral or written. A example of an oral summary is when you tell a friend about a movie or television show that you saw. A written summary is when you read a passage of text and then write down the main points.

Read a passage from your social studies textbook. Next, partner with a classmate, and briefly explain what you have learned from your reading. Have your partner do the same.

SOCIAL STUDIES ESSENTIAL SKILLS

Writing a Summary

Practice your summarizing skills by reading the passage below. When you are finished reading, close this book, and write down the key points from the passage in a brief paragraph. Make sure that you include all the important details and leave any unnecessary information out of your summary. Would a person who did not read this passage gain an understanding of Mount Rushmore from your summary?

Each year, about three million people visit Mount Rushmore. It is a national monument that honors four of the United States' greatest leaders. The massive sculpture is in the side of a mountain. The 60-foot-tall carvings are of the faces of four influential U.S. presidents. They are George Washington, Thomas Jefferson, Abraham Lincoln, and Theodore Roosevelt. Mount Rushmore was created by a sculptor named Gutzon Borglum. Borglum began working on the carvings in 1927, when he was 60 years old. He worked on Mount Rushmore for 14 years. Borglum died in 1941, before he was able to finish his work. His son, Lincoln, finished the monument on October 31, 1941.

Putting it All Together

A critical thinker uses many skills to solve problems and reach conclusions. These skills include evaluating, categorizing, comparing and contrasting, and summarizing. When critical thinkers have gathered all the needed information, they **synthesize** all of this knowledge to form an opinion or conclusion.

There are many different ways to synthesize information. Critical thinkers write essays or make a presentation to inform others about their opinions or conclusions. They also may create portfolios. A portfolio is a collection of items that proves a person has in-depth knowledge about a topic. Portfolios can include essays, artwork, tests, and other items that show the person knows a subject. A portfolio usually contains a written **reflection** of what a person learned and how he or she learned it.

Portfolios are a good way to demonstrate what you know about a subject.

Making a Portfolio

Think about a subject in school. Gather together examples of your best work from that subject. This can include tests, artwork, papers, and positive notes or comments from your teacher. You can also include items that you feel could be improved. Organize these pieces of work in a binder. Create a title page, and write a short introduction that tells other people what this portfolio represents.

Reflecting

Critical thinkers are never finished learning. When they have reached a conclusion or solution, critical thinkers reflect on what they have learned. This means that they think about how they reached their solutions. They also think about how they could have approached the problem differently. Reflecting helps improve critical thinking skills.

A good method for reflecting is to keep a journal. While working on a subject or project, write down what you learned and what you struggled with. Later, you can look back on your journal to better understand how you think during the learning process. Some teachers also keep journals. This helps them to understand the best ways that their students learn.

Have you ever written down the events that took place during your day? What types of things did you include? Try writing about your day today. What activities did you do? What did you learn from them?

Writing a Reflection

The following piece of writing reflects on a social studies topic.

During social studies, I learned about the American Revolution. I thought it was interesting to learn about all of the people involved. I wrote a paragraph about why the American Revolution happened, and I received a very good grade. It was hard to remember all of the dates when the battles took place. My teacher said it would help if I made a chart with all the battles listed in one column and the dates in another. I can read the chart every night before bed to help me remember when the battles happened.

Reflect on what you learned during a school project. Were there any areas that you struggled with? How do you plan to improve in these areas? You might find it difficult to remember dates for a history test. What can you do to remember them in the future? Now, write your thoughts in your notebook. This is a reflection.

Case Studies

A case study contains detailed information about a real-life problem and is usually presented like a story. Using a case study is a good way to improve critical thinking skills.

The people or characters in a case study face a problem that the reader of the case study must try to solve. The questions that are raised in a case study are usually open-ended questions. There can be many solutions to the problems that are presented.

You can use critical thinking skills such as evaluating and comparing and contrasting to solve case studies. For each solution, you should compare the pros and cons, or the advantages and the disadvantages, of the decision. Working in a group is a good way to solve a case study. Each group member can give opinions and bring different knowledge to the case study.

Think about a time when you had to make an important decision. How did you reach that decision? Did you think about the pros and cons of your actions?

A Real-Life Problem

Read the following case study. Can you think of more than one solution to Casey's problem? Then, use critical thinking skills such as identifying information, evaluating, categorizing, comparing and contrasting, and summarizing to determine which of your solutions is best. Think about what might happen to Casey depending on her decision.

Casey has been having trouble in her history class. The class has just finished a unit about the American Revolution. No matter how much she studies, Casey cannot remember all of the important events that happened during this period of history.

The night before the unit test, Casey studies for five hours. The next morning as Casey is walking to class, her friend Susan stops her in the hall. "Are you ready to get an 'A' on that test?" Susan asks. "I don't think so. I'm having trouble remembering everything," Casey says. "Don't worry," says Susan, bringing out a sheet of paper. "I have all of the answers right here."

Susan tells Casey she found the answers on their teacher's desk the previous day. She copied them down when the teacher was not in the room. "Here, copy them from me, and take them with you to the test. We'll both get 'A's!" says Susan. Casey looks at the paper. What should she do?

Put Your Knowledge to Use

Critical thinking is an important skill for social studies. It allows you to gather information and evaluate its importance and accuracy. This helps the critical thinker reach conclusions and solve problems.

1. **What is critical thinking?**

2. **What is the difference between a fact and an opinion?**

3. **What does it mean to compare and contrast two things?**

4. **Why is reflecting important?**

Answers:
1. Critical thinking is the process of improving the way a person thinks about a subject, statement, or idea.
2. A fact is something that is certain for everyone. It does not change, and it can be proven. An opinion is a view that a person has about a topic.
3. Comparing and contrasting means to think about how two or more things are alike and how they are different.
4. Reflecting helps you understand how you think during the learning process.

Websites for Further Research

There are many books and websites about critical thinking. To learn more about critical thinking, borrow books from the library, or surf the Internet.

Find out more about critical thinking skills by typing key words, such as "critical thinking," into the search field of your Web browser. There are many sites that help improve critical thinking skills.

Visit *www.criticalthinking.org* to learn more about critical thinking and why it is important. Click on "library/articles," and then click on "students."

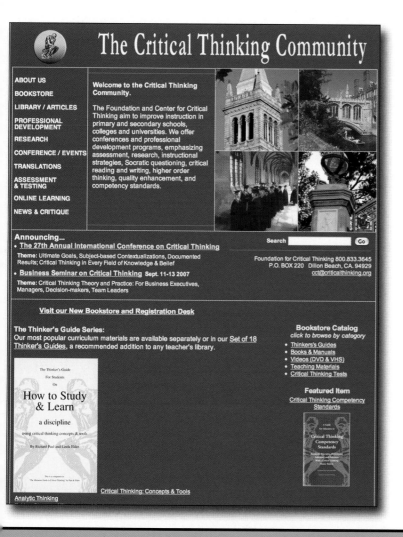

Glossary

American Revolution: a war fought from 1775–1783, in which the American colonies gained independence from Great Britain

bias: favoring one opinion compared to another

conclusion: the summarization of an argument

Constitution: the written set of laws that the government of the United States must follow

evaluate: to form an idea about the value of something

graphic organizer: a graph, chart, or table that shows data in a visual way

oath: a promise to act in a certain way

reflection: serious thought

summarize: express the main points of a large amount of information

synthesize: to combine many ideas into one main idea or conclusion

Index